Anger in the Bosom of our Children

Anger in the Bosom of our Children

The effects of fatherlessness on anger in middle school children

Cornelius Evans PhD

iUniverse, Inc.
New York Lincoln Shanghai

Anger in the Bosom of our Children
The effects of fatherlessness on anger in middle school children

All Rights Reserved © 2003 by Cornelius Evans, PhD

No part of this book may be reproduced or transmitted in any form or by any means, graphic, electronic, or mechanical, including photocopying, recording, taping, or by any information storage retrieval system, without the written permission of the publisher.

iUniverse, Inc.

For information address:
iUniverse, Inc.
2021 Pine Lake Road, Suite 100
Lincoln, NE 68512
www.iuniverse.com

ISBN: 0-595-30328-5

Printed in the United States of America

Contents

Chapter 1	THE CHANGING FAMILY IN AMERICA	1

- *The Importance of Family Structure* *1*
- *The Dramatic Increase in Fatherlessness* *2*
- *Differences Between Moms and Dads* *3*
- *Least Affected Groups* *4*

Chapter 2	PROBLEMS CAUSED BY THE ABSENT FATHER	6

- *Frightening Statistics* *6*
- *Impact of Fathers* *7*
- *Why Absent Dads Bring Negativity* *10*
- *Fathers and Middle School Children* *13*
- *Fathers and Daughters* *15*
- *Fathers and Sons* *17*
- *Gangs* *21*

Chapter 3	ANGER IN CHILDREN	23

- *How Absent Fathers Increase a Child's Anger* *24*
- *Other Reasons for Anger in Children* *26*
- *Signs of Anger* *30*
- *How Children Deal With Anger* *32*
- *Fatherlessness, Anger and Violence* *33*

Chapter 4	WHAT IT TAKES TO BE A GOOD FATHER	36

- *Caring* *36*
- *Sharing* *37*

- *Daring* *38*

CHAPTER 5   HELPING FATHERLESS CHILDREN COPE. 39
- *Identify the Reality of an Absent Father* *39*
- *Identify the Reality of the Primary Care Giver.* *40*
- *Actuate Morals by Modeling* *40*
- *Differentiate Reality of Family Structure.* *41*
- *Design Positive Program* *41*

CHAPTER 6   CONCLUSIONS AND IMPLICATIONS 42

REFERENCES 47

1

THE CHANGING FAMILY IN AMERICA

THE IMPORTANCE OF FAMILY STRUCTURE

The past 50 years have brought about a new awareness regarding the impact of families on the formation of personality, character, emotional reactions, and self-esteem (Brody, 1999). While it has always been known that individuals are strongly influenced by their families, experts now understand that the influence is far greater than anticipated in earlier years.

Families are dynamic social systems, with structural laws, components, and rules (Cadwick, et al, 1988). The most important of these family rules are those that determine what it means to be a human being. These rules embrace the most fundamental beliefs regarding raising children. The way that children are raised has been proven to form their core beliefs, attitudes, and emotional well-being.

This new awareness is not the only thing that has changed in the past 50 years. (Brody, 1999). Just a half century ago, raising a family in America without a father was rare. Over the past decades, this has changed drastically and many families are raised in a whole new way. In far too many families today, the father is missing in action. Overall, nearly four out of every ten children in America, approximately 24 million total, reside in a fatherless household.

With these new changes come many factors (Austin, et al., 1998). The rate of violence and anger in children has increased significantly during this time, as have the rates of teenage pregnancy, juvenile delinquency and drugs. All of these factors, when studied, have been somehow linked to adolescent problems that stem from the increase of absent fathers.

Children's needs are insatiable in the sense that they constantly need their parents throughout their childhood. Children who have been abandoned by their fathers often feel abandoned and alienated, which can create a shame-based or anger-based inner core.

Once a child's inner core is flawed by shame or anger, the experience of growing up and self-identity is painful. This is why many experts say that the root of shame and anger in children is primarily due to the absence of a father.

Experts are finding out that children, as they get older, need to establish contact with their biological father, even if they have a good stepfather. Boys need their fathers to teach them appropriate masculine behavior and to learn acceptable ways to deal with their feelings of aggression and how to relate to women. They need their fathers as good role models. Girls need their fathers to recognize and approve of them and to show that they think their daughters are worthwhile individuals.

THE DRAMATIC INCREASE IN FATHERLESSNESS

Dramatic increases in the number of children affected by divorce or being born out of wedlock has significantly altered the American family (Blackenhorn, 1995). In the early 1960s, nearly 90 percent of American children lived with both of their biological parents throughout their entire childhood.

Today, both biological parents raise less than half of all children. Nearly a third of these children are born to unmarried parents, most of whom never live together. Another third are the children of married parents who divorce sometime before the child becomes an adult. Additionally, many children are subjected to several marital disruptions and father figures, which can be intensely confusing.

DIFFERENCES BETWEEN MOMS AND DADS

The feminists' belief that there are no differences between men and women has proved to be false (Bumpass, et el., 1989). The natural instinct of mothers is to protect, comfort and nurture. They want their children, above all, to be happy, often at the expense of discipline. Traditionally, women spoil their children, especially their sons, and this lavishing needs to be balanced by less emotional and stricter fathers. Mothers yearn to be loved, and fathers want to be obeyed. It is men who teach their sons to control their aggression, and, in the end, to respect women.

Freud says that children will alternate between feelings of gratification and frustration in their search for father, a powerful drive object that is "lost" and must be "found." "Lost" in this context, refers to a period in the child's life when it has identified father as significant and has noticed that he is not always present (Levine, 1995). Freud believed that this struggle to find father produced an early form of "picture-thinking" (Levine). The child tried desperately to form and hold his father's image. His inaccessibility was the very quality, which singled out father for such special treatment in the child's development. As children develop, they often have to cope with father-absence, which is real and possibly permanent. Reasons for a father's absence include these: divorce or separation, death, desertion, work commitments away from home, military service, illness, and imprisonment.

There is also another kind of father-absence in which father is physically present in the family, yet is unavailable, probably because he fears intimacy in relating and habitually uses behavioral defenses, such as anger and coldness, to escape it.

Erikson believes that the child will judge parents from the standpoint of an immature Superego, lacking judgment and discernment. Before this inner tribunal, parents can be condemned as tricksters who proclaim moral laws but manage to escape from what the child sees as proper punishment (Lupton, et al, 1997).

The child's attitude towards his parents can contain a mixture of love, need and a strong sense of resentment. The absent father, easily labeled as the deserter, can be mourned, needed and rejected all at the same time. I have seen this resentment projected onto other significant figures in later life, from where it sours relationships in the here-and-now and prevents healing of past wounds.

While mature, sensible mothers have proven capable of successfully rearing children into adulthood, it is inevitable that, when their father is absent, children do lose advantages such as varied interaction, richness of family connectedness, witnessing the very male-female relationship that gave them life.

LEAST AFFECTED GROUPS

Since black and Hispanic children tend to come from less advantaged backgrounds than white children, their underlying risk of behavioral problems, such as anger and aggression, is higher. Therefore, many experts say that the effect of family disruption should be greater on blacks and Hispanic children than on white children (Haveman, et al., 1994). However, due to the fact that single motherhood is more common and accepted in black and Hispanic communities, many experts argue that the effect of fatherlessness on minority children should be smaller than the effect on white children.

After studying several reports, it appears that the absence of a father decreases the success of white children more than any other racial and ethnic group. The absence of a father increases both the school failure risk and behavioral problem risk among African Americans and Hispanics by 75 percent and 96 percent respectively (Haveman, 1994).

The absence of a father appears to cancel out the educational and behavioral advantage of being white. White children from one-parent households are significantly more likely to drop out than blacks from two-parent homes, and they are nearly as likely to experience school failure and behavioral problems as blacks from similarly disrupted families.

2

PROBLEMS CAUSED BY THE ABSENT FATHER

FRIGHTENING STATISTICS

Changes in family life have led to numerous research projects and studies regarding the consequences of absent fathers. Many analysts say that growing up without a father is the primary cause of many of America's social problems, including anger in children, poverty, dropping out of school, truancy, and delinquency (Popenoe, 1988).

According to statistics, child well-being over the past thirty years has deteriorated significantly. Juvenile violent crime has increased six times, from 16,000 arrests in 1960 to 96,000 in 1992, a period in which the total number of juveniles in the population remained relatively stable.

- Reports of child neglect and abuse have quintupled since 1976, when data were first collected.

- Eating disorders and rates of depression have soared among adolescent girls.

- Teen suicide has tripled.

- SAT scores have declined nearly 80 points.

- Poverty has shifted from the elderly to the young. Of the entire nation's poor today, 38 percent are children.

- Evidence is now strong that the loss of fathering is the most prominent reason for all of these conditions, independent of economic issues (Austin, et al., 1998).

IMPACT OF FATHERS

Fathers have an extraordinary impact on the lives of their children—sometimes positive, sometimes negative (Popenoe, 1998). In 1995, nearly 25 million children were living in homes without their biological fathers. About 40% of those children had not seen their fathers in at least a year; 50% had never been in their fathers' homes. By 1996, 60% of black children, 19% of white children and 30% of Hispanic children lived in homes without a father. A study of 22,000 children ages 12 to 17 found that adolescent girls in mother-only families were nearly twice as likely to use illegal drugs, alcohol or tobacco as girls living with both biological parents (Popenoe, 1996).

Today's generation of adolescents is fatherless because of a variety of circumstances, including abandonment, divorce, and busy lifestyles. The result of this absence of fathers is a generation of lonely, angry, and hurting children who are raised without the love, strength, protection, encouragement, and the discipline of a father.

In the United States in 2000, two out of every five children did not live with their fathers (Manski, et al., 1992). Half of single mothers reported that they saw no value in the father's contact with their children. This means that millions of American children live without a father and forty percent of these children have not seen their dads in over a year. These children show their anger and loneliness in many ways. Of all high school dropouts, 71 percent did not have a father at home while growing up. In addition, 85 percent of all juvenile delinquent home inmates were from fatherless homes.

A recent report created by a group of pediatricians revealed that preschool children being raised by a single parent are more likely to be slower in developmental progress and skills such as toilet training.

(Popenoe, 1996). They are also more likely to develop disorders of sleeping and eating. In addition, these small children have a tendency to develop acute separation anxiety and fear of abandonment by both parents. The report also revealed that middle-school children from single parent homes are more likely than children with two parents to show symptoms of anger, sadness, and depression. They also tend to blame themselves or their parents for their loss or, in some cases, deny or ignore the loss. The report states that these children are withdrawn and often daydream. They also may have poor grades, be aggressive, and show signs of anti-social behavior, such as violence and anger.

Most studies agree that children with absent biological fathers do less well than children who grow up with both natural parents (Austin, et al., 1998). These children tend to exhibit discipline problems early in life, often lashing out against their peers and authority figures. Later in life, the problems grow. These children are less likely to finish high school, find a steady job, and a niche in society. They are more likely to end up in jail or become teenage mothers. However, many reports say that the numbers are not significant enough to support the claim that a father's absence is the major cause of social problems amongst American children, such as anger and delinquency. Despite the fact that children with absentee fathers are more likely to have behavioral problems than children with two parents, the difference in numbers is not great. Many children who grow up without a father do just fine, according to reports.

For example, Judith Stacey, a sociologist critical of the fatherhood movement, argues, "Access to economic, educational, and social resources, the quality and consistency of parental nurturance, guidance, and responsibility affect child development and welfare far more substantially than does the particular number…and actual marital status of parents or the family structure in which children are reared." What Stacey does not mention, however, is that it is the married two-parent family that is the family structure best equipped to provide children with these resources (Blankenhorn, 1995).

Psychologist Louise Silverstein argues that it is not fathers, but "the stability of the emotional connection and the predictability of the care taking relationship that are the significant variables that predict positive child adjustment." However, this stability and predictability is most likely to occur in a married two-parent family (Hanson, 1997).

Some other critics of these research reports argue that the absence of a father does not condemn a child to psychiatric problems, educational failure, drug addiction, and a life of crime. These critics say that the majority of children from fatherless families and stepfamilies turn out fine.

Also, according to opponents of these studies, marriage is not a guarantee of good parenting, and high-conflict or abusive fathers can be far worse for children than no father at all. Overall, they say, there is no evidence that father absence harms the majority of children who experience it.

This is true, often because of the extraordinary efforts of single mothers. Still, the differences between children in one and two-parent families are not so small as to be inconsequential, and there is fairly good evidence that father absence is responsible for at least some of them.

It is a proven fact that father absence presents a serious risk factor for children. Just as smoking cigarettes may not badly harm the majority of those who have ever smoked, it does harm many (Beck, 1988). Similarly, a child who grows up without an involved father is much more likely to suffer disadvantages and other negative psychological effects.

Children who grow up in fatherless homes are five times more likely to be poor (Blankenhorn, 1995). This fact provides strong evidence that fatherlessness causes poverty. It is also true that poverty contributes to father absence. Unemployed or underemployed men are less likely to get married than men with stable, well-paying jobs. Therefore, economic instability often leads to family instability. It is a vicious cycle.

WHY ABSENT DADS BRING NEGATIVITY

Growing up without a father negatively affects children for three reasons: A family without a father typically has fewer financial resources to devote to children's upbringing and education, less time and energy to nurture and supervise children, and reduced access to community resources that can supplement and support parents' efforts.

Fatherless homes create an atmosphere that places children at a higher risk of violence and gang activity. The need to belong to something is transferred from the family to the gang.

According to the National Center of Health Statistics, children who are raised without a father are 75 percent more likely to need help with emotional problems and twice as likely to repeat a grade in school (Poponoe, 1996).

"Sixty-three percent of youth suicides are from fatherless homes. Ninety percent of all homeless and runaway children are from fatherless homes; 85 percent of children that exhibit behavior disorders come from fatherless homes," says Tom Hoerner, author of *Bachelor Parents and Their Functional Families*.

While many experts are convinced that other factors in this country, such as increases in drugs, violence and poverty, are contributing to anger in school children, statistics show similar trends in fatherless children in other countries, such as Canada.

A statistics Canada studied reported 23,000 children across the country during an eight-month period in 1994 and 1995 were affected. The central conclusion of the study is that children that were raised by single mothers face increased risks of emotional, behavioral, academic and social problems. (Statistics Canada) One in six children in Canada live in single-parent families, 93 percent of these headed by single mothers.

Social researchers have long known that growing up in poverty puts children at higher risk for problems such as hyperactivity, emotional distress or failing a grade at school. But, the report showed the incidence of such problems among children of well-off single mothers was generally higher than for children from poor two-parent families.

A recent Men Against Violence survey reveals that:

- 85 percent of all children that exhibit behavioral disorders come from fatherless homes.

- 71 percent of all high school dropouts come from fatherless homes.

- 75 percent of all adolescent patients in chemical abuse centers come from fatherless homes.

- 70 percent of juveniles in state operated institutions come from fatherless homes.

- 85 percent of all youths sitting in prisons grew up in fatherless homes.

- 80 percent of rapists motivated with displaced anger come from fatherless homes.

- 90 percent of all homeless and runaway children are from fatherless homes (Poponoe, 1996).

These statistics translate to mean that children from a fatherless home are:

- 20 times more likely to have behavioral disorders

- 9 times more likely to drop out of high school

- 10 times more likely to abuse chemical substances

- 9 times more likely to end up in state operated institutions

- 20 times more likely to end up in prison
- 10 times more likely to commit rape
- 32 times more likely to run away from home (San Francisco Chronicle, 1995)

According to another study, adolescents who grow up in homes without fathers are twice as likely to end up in jail as those who come from traditional two-parent families. The study shows that boys whose fathers were absent from the household had double the odds of being incarcerated, even when other factors such as race, income, parent education and urban residence were constant.

In addition, the study, which aims to shed light on the increase in youth violence, shows that boys who grow up with a stepfather in the home were at even higher risk for incarceration, roughly three times that of children who remain with both of their natural parents. This indicates that a stepfather does not erase the problem of an absent father.

The study also found that young children whose parents part ways during their adolescence were roughly one and one-half times as likely to end up in jail as children from intact families.

Concern about youth violence in our community has become the focus of many government and community leaders. Violence in youth is a troubling sign that many of this country's youth are not developing appropriately.

The ability of youth to live and learn in a safe environment has become a priority of both parents and the community. Because of the ever-changing structure of families and the roles that educators are asked to play in the lives of their students, it is important to look at the issue of youth violence.

There are many factors that may contribute to youth violence. Lack of parental involvement in student, school, and domestic activities may contribute to school violence. Poor academic performance, which leads to poor self-esteem, is a major predictor of delinquency in school-aged children.

There is also a strong correlation between children and domestic abuse and juvenile violence in our community. In addition, societal standards have disintegrated, creating a moral crisis and generally desensitizing our youth toward violence.

"Adolescents speak out about their Fathers," a study done at New York University in 1996, consists of a conclusion gathered from interviews of 45 school-aged girls who grew up in fatherless homes (Coltrane, 1996). Of the total, 33% of the girls felt conflicted or enraged. One girl reported that she was very angry with her absent dad yet felt emotionally attached to him. In the report, Ken Rigby wrote, "Positive self-esteem and emotional well being have been seen to a rise in families characterized by warmth and parental attention; anger and aggressive behavior among children has been seen to arise from family that are cold and disconnected."

Female adolescents raised in fatherless homes tend to be associated with lower self-esteem, precocious sexual activity, greater delinquent-like behavior, and more difficulty establishing gratifying, lasting adult heterosexual relationships.

Children need self-assurance, love, and praise from both a father and mother. Without a father, girls turn that pain inward and feel they are inadequate and undeserving of love. Often, they feel that their dads are absent because of them. Without a father, girls become emotionally dependent on others for the lack of love and masculine example that they should have gotten from their dads.

FATHERS AND MIDDLE SCHOOL CHILDREN

Father structure and father involvement have long been the basis of research regarding the importance of fathers in the lives of middle-school children. (Hanson, 1996). Family structure studies focus on children who live in families with single mothers and the analysis of how these children fare in comparison to children living with two-parent families on a variety of indices. The following studies present interesting statistics on father absence.

The 1988 National Health Interview Survey revealed that children without fathers were more vulnerable to illness. The report showed that children who live apart from their biological father had 20 to 30 percent health vulnerability ratios and 50 percent higher incidence of asthma (Griswold, 1993).

An 18-year longitudinal study of all newborns born to single mothers indicated that, at the age of fifteen, these children were 4.3 times more likely to smoke. This was the strongest association seen in a multivariate analysis which included many other variables including residence, mobility, ethnicity, SES, family size, etc. (McLanahan, et al., 1994).

The National Household Educational Survey of 1996 stated that children who grew up with attentive fathers were: more likely to get good grades; less likely to repeat a grade; less likely to be expelled; more likely to enjoy school; and more likely to participate in extracurricular activities (Griswold, 1993).

Additional studies show that even in high crime neighborhoods, 90 percent of kids from safe, stable two-parent homes do not become delinquents. In addition, these children are less likely to become sexually active at a very young age.

These factors strongly suggest that the absence of a father has a tremendous influence on children. If these fatherless children are having premarital sex, getting in trouble and doing poorly in school, it is obvious that they have psychological issues, such as anger or depression that is leading to these actions.

FATHERS AND DAUGHTERS

In Jonetta Rose Barras' book, *Whatever Happened to Daddy's Little Girl? The Impact of Fatherlessness on Black Women,* the author discusses fatherless daughters, especially African-Americans. The author says that often fatherlessness is passed down from generation to generation like a disease or a family heirloom. Barras stated that the reason for the absence of the father does not matter. It could be the father's death, the parents divorcing, a workaholic father, or a father who is so emotionally withdrawn that he does not display any care, attention, or affection toward his daughter. The daughter interprets this absence as rejection or abandonment and wonders why she was expelled from her father's life and denied his presence. The best answer that her immaturity can come up with is that she is not worthy of her father's attention, or that she is in some manner defective or unlovable, or that she is deficient in some quality her father admires. She blames herself and promptly proceeds to hide the pain. Burying the pain and at the same time wishing to earn her father's attention she compromises her integrity, her sense of worth, and her self-esteem-in other words, her very sense of self. The pain, says the author, which is the consequence concomitant with the sense of loss, becomes the prime mover of her entire existence. This pain and lacking defines and controls virtually every facet of her life.

Barras implies that the fatherless daughter often reacts at a young age with aggression or suspicion to various situations. Everything in the young girl's world becomes tainted with the potential of another loss, more pain, and a greater void.

The author says that fatherless daughters experience rage, anger, and depression as the result of their abandonment. Rage, she states, is anger turned outward, and could be a power for positive, constructive achievement or negative, destructive violence. Depression is the result of anger turned inward.

According to Barras, "a girl abandoned by the first man in her life forever entertains powerful feelings of being unworthy or incapable of receiving any man's love. Even when she receives love from another, she is constantly and intensely fearful of losing it. This is the anxiety, the pain, of losing one father. I had had three fathers toss me aside; the cumulative effect was catastrophic."

Barras does not believe that it is possible for a girl to escape a fatherless home without scars.

> Your family is your first social interactive group. It's the foundation. When that foundation has cracks or holes, you'd better know that your springing into society is not going to be the same as it would have been. This is the reality. If I walk with one broken heel, I'm not going to have an even walk.

Since fathers teach girls how to relate to men and to maneuver in a male dominated society, Barras says, girls without fathers grow up not understanding relationships with members of the opposite sex.

"Fathers help their daughters become comfortable as to who they are as a girl and later as a woman," she writes. "They help you negotiate in the real world. We are still living in a fairly masculine world, and we need men to help us understand that masculinity. We need men to help us understand what it is to be a man.

"Without those early lessons from a father figure, women are at great risk. "If it is true that a father helps to develop his daughter's confidence in herself and in her femininity, that he helps her to shape her style and understanding of male-female bonding, and that he introduces her to the external world, plotting navigational courses for her success, then surely it is an indisputable conclusion that the absence of these lessons can produce a severely wounded and disabled woman," she writes.

Women whose fathers were physically present but "emotionally unavailable," Barras says, also may "express many of the symptoms of the fatherless woman syndrome." She describes them as:

- The "un" factor. Feeling unworthy and unlovable. "Fatherless women are sure, absolutely sure, no one would really want them, not one could love them. When it does appear that they have won love…there has got to be some hitch; it's a trick."

- The triple fear factor. Fear of rejection, abandonment and commitment. The fatherless woman reaches out for someone but believes he will leave, so she runs away. Often, she will play it safe, avoiding any deep relationship for fear of the ultimate rejection.

- The sexual healing factor. Sexual expression, from promiscuity to an aversion to intimacy. Often, women "go from man to man, from bed to bed, calling sex 'love' and hoping to be healed by the physical closeness."

- The "over" factor. The powerful need to overcompensate and overachieve. Striving for perfection is "the fatherless daughter's way of announcing to the father who left her that it is his loss," says Barras. "We are at the top of our class. We break the glass ceilings." But it is simply a shield, a tool designed to prevent anyone from getting close enough to see the despair." If that doesn't produce the desired effect, she says, many women "oversaturate" with food, drugs, alcohol, sex or work.

- The RAD factor. Rage, anger, depression. The rage can take the form of a fierce drive to succeed, or it can be expressed in addiction, criminal activity, child abuse or depression—rage turned inward.

FATHERS AND SONS

There is a great deal of research that shows that the breakdown in modern families, which often results in fatherlessness, has a serious effect on male children. The family's imbalance has been proven to be detrimental to the self-identity and achievements of many boys and directly related to feeling of anger in young boys.

For as long as humans have been breathing, thinking beings, two committed parents have been viewed as important factors in the healthy and balanced development of a child. An uninterested, a part-time or an absent parent can have a detrimental effect on their children as they learn and grow.

"Boy Troubles," a study that looks into the puzzling differences between girls and boys in crime occurrences, school performance, and rates of suicide, indicates that strong families and sound parenting are vital factors in the protecting of children in their growth to adulthood (Blankenhorn, 1999). According to the study, "Girls commit only a fraction of the crimes that boys do; their school performance is better and outpacing boys; and they do not commit suicide at anything like the rate of boys."

The incidence of juvenile crime has sharply increased over the last 20 years, much of it due to increasing offenses by young males. The majority of juvenile crimes are committed by a smaller group of frequent offenders, mostly boys.

While there is a spectrum of risk factors that give rise to juvenile crime, it is clear that child neglect, incompetent parenting, or an inadequate parent-child relationship can result in anti-social behavior that leads to delinquency or chronic or criminal behavior. The evidence shows that strong families and sound parenting are the most important factors in protecting children from juvenile crime and long term offending.

There has also been a significant deterioration in the school performance of boys. "Up until the early 1990s, the average school performance of boys and girls was close to equal. Since then, the gender gap favoring girls has widened each year," according to the study. "Boys are now said to be 'disadvantaged' in relation to girls." Socio-economic factors often affect school performance but boys and girls can experience this equally. Broken families, with absent fathers, appear to affect boys more than girls.

The discussion on young male suicide is shocking. Suicide is the leading cause of death in young males between 15 to 24 years. In 1997, more young male deaths in that age bracket were from suicide, rather than road traffic accidents. Again, there are many risk factors leading to this, but family structure and relationships, and parental role models are discussed. The study says:

> For boys particularly, the absence of a father in the home is a deprivation. Whether we like it or not, it still makes sense to speak of a masculine culture and of ideals of manhood to which most boys aspire, be it consciously or unconsciously. Boys look for models and guidance from the men and other boys with whom they have contact. But if such contact is devoid of strength of character, or if it is emotionally and morally "thin", a developmental influence of the greatest importance will be missing or misdirected (Blankenhorn).

Boys tend to experience the following:

- Difficulty in resolving rivalry issues

- Deprivation of a same-sex role model

- Tendency to act out stress with violence

- Physical symptoms in response to stress

- Aggression toward their mothers

- Mother transferring to the son her negative attitudes toward the father

- Pressure to assume the role of supporter and head of household

The male children of absent fathers are at a greater risk of acting out in school and getting in trouble with the police.

According to Dr. David Popenoe, professor of sociology at Rutgers University: "Teenage boys without fathers are notoriously prone to trouble. The pathway to adulthood for daughters is somewhat easier, but they still must learn from their fathers, as they cannot from their mothers, how to relate to men. They learn from their fathers about heterosexual trust, intimacy, and difference. They learn to appreciate their own femininity from the one male who is most special in their lives. Most important, through loving and being loved by their fathers, they learn that they are worthy of love" (McLanahan).

Studies show that the absence of a father is a more important predictor of youth violence than skin color, income, education "level," or the quality of the neighborhood. Fathers are the most important figure in showing a boy what it means to be a man. According to studies, when a child is raised without a father, there is a prevalent hate for authority. This makes sense, as the father is one of the first authority figures in a child's life. Teachers and single mothers bear the brunt of this hatred for authority. Middle-school aged children will often blatantly disobey orders, challenging authority. Deep anger is resident in kids where rejection is experienced early on. If a child's father is absent, he/she often feels personally rejected, leading to this deep anger.

There are often few male influences in a child's life when there is no father figure in the house. While 100 years ago, only males could teach elementary school, today 90 percent of the teachers are women. More than 80 percent of child custody cases go to the mother, and 95 percent daycare workers are female. Therefore, many boys grow up with little or no male influence in their lives. In these cases, the important role that men play in the lives of boys is never realized. Robert Bly in his book *Iron John* says, "When a father and son spend long hours together we could say that a substance almost like food passes from the older body to the younger (Bly).

"The son's body, not his mind, receives, and the father gives this food at a level far below consciousness. His cells receive some knowledge of what an adult masculine body is. The younger body learns at what frequency the masculine body vibrates. It begins to grasp the song that adult male cells sing." Manhood is something that cannot be taught by a book or movie; it must be passed on.

Studies show that fatherless boys are at greater risk for depression than those in intact families. Boys look to their fathers to teach them and provide an example for them. Fatherless boys show more signs of higher frequencies than boys with fathers of dependency, irrelevant talk, withdrawal, blaming, and inattention, as well as decreased work effort and higher frequencies of inappropriate behavior and unhappiness.

GANGS

Many experts agree that the increase of gangs in America is directly related to the absence of fathers. The absence of a father burdens the single mother with the role of both mom and dad, which is overwhelming and impossible.

The typical single mother is overloaded with obligations, including raising the children, fixing meals, housekeeping, getting the children to school and home, keeping track of health and doctor's visits, assisting with homework and problems, and making sure that all bills are paid (Levine, 1995).

After performing all these tasks, the single mother is left with little time for nurturing her children and caring for herself. It is a fact that many single mothers have absolutely no outlets for relieving stress. This can affect their children in many ways, as mothers who are exhausted often neglect the emotional needs of their children.

Even if a father does not treat his children properly or ignores them, children still seek their father's approval. Particularly for young boys, a father's approving glances and remarks are critical for the development of his children. Boys crave approval and unconditional love from their dads, as well as guidance and respect. Without this approval and support, children feel lost.

The feeling of being lost could influence the child to become a delinquent. The rise of juvenile delinquency and violence is at an all time high in my general environment. Juvenile delinquency and violence are clearly generated disproportionately by youths in mother-only households and in other households where the biological father is not present (Popenoe, 1996). Accordingly, a statistical review of fifty major studies on the effects of family structure on delinquency concluded that "the effect of intact versus 'broken' families is a consistent and real pattern of association…the prevalence of delinquency in broken homes is 10-15 percent higher than in intact homes (Popenoe). Children from broken homes are at a higher risk of becoming a gang member than those children that are not. Evidence that fatherless children are more driven to become gang members is shown in this general population at an enormous rate. The proliferations of gangs are sweeping the country like never before. The involvement can no longer be seen as an inner city or social-economic problem. Gang violence has penetrated even the wealthiest communities. The fact that the father's love is absent in most cases causes juveniles (middle school children) to seek attention in other places, preferably gangs.

3

ANGER IN CHILDREN

Anger is an emotion that is closely connected with survival instinct. People use anger as a tool to protect themselves from harm and prepare themselves for action. Author Harville Hendrix describes anger as "the other side of hurt, shame, and humiliation—emotions and experiences that also stir the survival instinct." Hendrix says, "If anger were always suppressed, passion would atrophy, and our children could become victims of many dangerous circumstances" (Brody, 1999).

Anger is always a secondary emotion that is precipitated by emotions such as hurt, fear or frustration. Anger is an immediate response to these emotions. For many fatherless children, it is easy to focus on the anger and overlook the underlying issues.

Often, anger can be positive and useful. It is a means of protection and a signal that something is wrong. However, Hendrix notes, "When uncontained, anger sabotages a desired outcome" (Brody).

Typically, it is this uncontained, sabotaging anger that causes alarm among parents and teachers of an angry child.

Psychologists say that the single most effective method of teaching children about dealing with anger is by example. Parents are advised to set a good example about managing anger and teach those skills to their children, by example and by relating specific information. However, without a father, children do not get the example they need and often do not know how to manage their anger problems.

To gain attention, power, and revenge and/or display inadequacy, children often use uncontained anger as a tool (Barber, et al., 2000).

This inadequacy may come from the lack of a father and the need for revenge may stem from blame of the mother.

With the absence of a father, children may feel one or more of the following: shock, disbelief, fear, guilt, grief, confusion, shame, loss, and anger. These reactions are often closely linked and may be hard to separate. Children often have trouble understanding and talking about their feelings, which leads to added stress and anger.

The intensity and ways that fatherless children express their reactions vary greatly depending on their personal experience, general mental health, other stress factors in their lives, their coping style, their ability to self-monitor their emotional state, and their support network.

For many children without a father, anger is a natural extension of other emotions because it is a defensive mechanism that makes them feel more in control. In many ways, anger with their absent fathers is justified. The absence of a father is bringing them pain and the loss of important lessons. Their desire to retaliate can be strong, especially since they do not have a concrete enemy to focus their anger on. Since their father is not present, these children often direct their feelings toward their mothers, peers and teachers. They may lash out at classmates or neighbors because they cannot lash out at their father.

How Absent Fathers Increase a Child's Anger

It is important to examine the reasons why the lack of a father would increase a child's feelings of anger. First of all, when fathers live away from their children or are non-existent in their lives, they are less likely to contribute monetarily to the child (Gafinkel, et al., 1994). Therefore, children without fathers tend to have a lower standard of living than they would have if they had the income of their father and mother.

About half of the disadvantage of father absence is mainly because of economic insecurity and instability. Another quarter is because of the loss of parental time and supervision, and the rest is most likely due to a loss of social capital attributable in large measure to the higher incidence of residential mobility among single mothers and remarried mothers.

In many of America's inner cities, the rate of fatherless families exceeds 80 percent (McLanahan, et al., 1989). Children in these families are seven times more likely to be poor and three times more predisposed to behavioral and emotional problems. Without fathers, it is more likely that they get pregnant as adolescents, never finish high school, experience divorce later in life, and become victims of violence.

Illegitimacy is one of the leading causes of fatherlessness. Forty percent of births in America are to single mothers. Among minorities, this figure increases up to 70 percent. It is 30 percent in the white population. Illegitimacy is the most important social problem because it leads to so many of the other problems in our communities, and the desertion of fathers is linked to many factors, among which are irresponsibility and invisibility.

Parents' authority is measured by many things: whether they know their children's whereabouts, whether they leave them home alone, whether they establish a curfew, and whether they set rules for television watching, bedtime, and household chores. Many studies demonstrate that single mothers exercise less control over their children than their still-married peers.

The difference is particularly great when comparing married mothers, with never-married mothers or mothers with a live-in partner. More than 30 percent of two-parent families report never leaving a child home alone, in contrast with 20.4 percent of mothers with partners and 19.3 percent of never-married mothers (McLanahan). Remarried mothers report about the same level of supervision as mothers in two-parent families.

OTHER REASONS FOR ANGER IN CHILDREN

Media and Community

In today's society, anger and violence are everywhere. (Brody, 1999). During the average child's childhood, he will witness 100,000 acts of violence in the media. Most psychologists say that children are affected by this media violence. Additionally, children are influenced by violence in the streets. Therefore, if they are raised in bad neighborhood, it will affect them, also.

Family Life

Many experts say that the majority of angry and violent children come from families that are angry and violent. These families teach their children by example, so their children are likely to exhibit violent, abusive, and aggressive behavior. This is the result of weak family bonding, little warmth and nurturing, and family attitudes favorable to drug usage and crime.

Dr. Cathy Widom has studied a group of abused and neglected children since 1988. She believes that severe abuse and neglect are predictive of violent behavior in children. Her research includes stories of violent children with complex partial seizures, negative symptoms, and a background of horrible abuse and violence.

If the adults in their lives solve problems with anger or in a violent manner then that is what the child will do. Statistically, we know that 79 percent of violent children have witnessed violence between their parents and that violent children are four times more likely to come from homes with parental violence.

Problems in School

Many children become angry or violent due to learning problems in middle school. They may be embarrassed or frustrated about their difficulties in learning, resulting in frequent absence, truancy, and aggression in the classroom. These problems will follow them for their entire lives.

Peer-Related Issues

Children, like adults, have a strong need for success and positive self-worth. When these children fail to find these things, they tend to look for other youth with similar problems and views. This is how children form packs or gangs.

Attachment Disorders

When children fail to develop primary attachment bonds, this can result in violence, lack of empathy, and lack of control. Statistics show that 800,000 children with severe attachment disorders are coming to the attention of the child welfare system every year.

Boys who experience attachment problems early in life are three times more likely to be violent. Eighty percent of maltreated children show disorganized-disoriented attachment patterns, resulting in children who are impulsive, full of rage, out of control, and violent.

Psychological Issues

Violent children often tend to be those that modulate aggressive behavior. Children with severe brain damage due to accidents and deliberate abuse are likely to exhibit angry and aggressive behavior. Many aggressive and violent children have borderline intellectual functioning.

Poor Communication Skills

Typically, angry children experience little emotion other than violent and angry feelings. If one or both parents are unavailable, children do not learn how to communicate feelings. Violent children often bottle things up until they simply explode with rage. Their lack of bonding leaves them lacking in interpersonal skills and they do not understand the basic trust necessary for normal human relationships.

Poor Self-Image

Children who view themselves in a negative way often see the world as a dangerous place and feel that they must fight for survival. They also tend to feel that everyone is critical of them and respond to this with anger.

Antisocial Behavior and Drugs

Anger and violence of youth have been proven to stem from children who have had early and persistent antisocial behavior beginning with minor behavior problems around age seven. This progresses to moderate problems at about age nine and serious behavior problems around age 11 to 12. Violent children are often drug and alcohol abusers, and many times, they come from substance abusing families.

Lack of Moral Development

Many angry or violent children fail in the earlier stages of moral development. Children who do not progress morally often think egocentrically. In order to grow up emotionally healthy, children need constant, positive, and nurturing caregivers who set rules, respect a child's individuality and provide secure attachment.

Violence In Schools

Violence in schools has spread widely throughout the nation. This has caused many problems among students, families, faculty of schools, and residents of the areas. Violence in schools affects many men, women, and children in our country. The types of violence seen today include fistfights, sexual abuse, threats, and gun shootings. These are just a few examples of the many types of violence that are happening in schools today.

Experts have cited many reasons for the increase of school violence. Some are blaming a breakdown of "educational standards and behavior," while others are noting problems within a child's family. Still others are blaming the increase of the availability of children getting their hands on some type of firearm.

The American family is a major concern when looking at statistics of violence in children. More and more children are born to women who are not married. This may cause abused, neglected, troubled kids.

Almost three-fourths of the United States teens are afraid of violent crime amongst their peers. Violence in schools has become a big problem in current society. With all the people being injured or killed in schools by guns and other weapons, more and more people are getting more weapons to bring into schools. Nearly half of all males and one-third of all students say that they can easily obtain a handgun if they desire to.

Carrying guns and other weapons around schools is becoming more and more popular all around the world. Children, in middle and high school, think that carrying guns around schools with them will make them cool or fit in with other people like themselves.

Security has become a big part of schools today. An increasing number of schools have been getting metal detectors installed. The New York City public schools report that since the introduction to metal detectors in 1988, serious incidents have declined by 58% in schools with scanners and by 43% without them.

Teachers and students are both in danger of being killed or attacked at school in today's society. The risk of a teacher being attacked by a student has doubled since 1956.

This violence in school is stemming from numerous problems, including the increased number of absent fathers. Children today simply are not getting the attention, support, and skills that they need to grow up as responsible human beings.

Signs of Anger

The following have been identified as signs of anger in children:

- Behavioral outbursts, many times without an obvious cause
- Sleep problems
- Fights at school or home
- Physical attacks on others or animals
- Disobedience from otherwise well-behaved children
- Child says he or she is sad and does not know why

- Complaints of physical ailments (Blankenhorn, 1995) The following have been identified as signs of extreme emotional trauma:

- Disruption in peer relationships (little or no interactions with friends, significant increase in conflict with classmates or friends)

- Strained family relationships (high degree of misbehavior, lashing out against family members, refusal to participate in normal family routines)

- Significant decrease in school performance

- Ongoing physical complaints with no apparent cause

- Use of chemicals, alcohol (or increase in comparison to previous behavior)

- Repetitive play re-enacting the traumatic events

- Low self esteem, negative talk about self (if this was not apparent prior to the trauma)

- General lack of energy and lack of interest in previously enjoyed activities (Blankenhorn, 1995).

Many single mothers do not understand why their children become so angry at such a young age. They do not realize the importance of a father in teaching children the basic rules or how to manage their anger.

Many psychologists blame anger in children on many sources. Some say that anger is hereditary and is one of the reasons that humans are the dominant species today. Anger was a way to defend our territory, feed our families, and protect us from harm. Aggressive early man accomplished this and passed the traits on from generation to generation. Others say that the root of anger is in humanity and that anger is a survival mechanism, notifying us that something is wrong. To a certain extent, anger is healthy; it defines us, and provides a means for action. Children may encounter a frustrating situation and react by becoming angry. Anger in and of itself may not change the situation, but the emotion propels the child to react. Some psychologists look into physical details for reasons for anger. In the child plagued by fatigue, sleep deprivation, or pain? Often high sugar diets can contribute to angry responses (Haveman, et al, 1994). While these things are not the root cause of anger, they do contribute and may trigger an angry response. Many professionals also feel that the way children view or perceive an event will determine how they react. Everyone interprets events differently because our senses pick up different stimuli.

HOW CHILDREN DEAL WITH ANGER

Angry children create situations for themselves that seem to perpetuate the anger. Children who are chronically angry and lash out aggressively, hitting, starting fights, or verbal arguments, tend to create negative reactions from others. Friends, siblings, and classmates may assume that the angry child is going to react angrily to a situation, and thus avoid him. These children have poor anger-management skills, resulting in poor social skills, and need additional help learning how do deal with their anger.

Chronic stress, such as dealing with an absent father, reduces a child's ability to remain calm and cope with everyday frustrations. Children know that something is wrong within the family and may see that they are not like other families.

Angry children are those who tend to react to troubles with anger, blame others for their own problems, and are not very good at understanding their own feelings or the feelings of others. They also may have a difficult time analyzing problems in ways that would lead to peaceful solutions.

Increasingly, evidence has shown that children who do not know their fathers feel rejected, abandoned and angry. Children need fathers because the two sexes bring totally different strengths to parenthood.

FATHERLESSNESS, ANGER AND VIOLENCE

According to research gathered by the National Fatherhood Initiative, the proportion of fatherless households in a community predicts its rate of violent crime and burglary, while the community's poverty level does not (Hanson, 1996). In adolescent cases, 72% of adolescent murderers, 60% of rapists, and 39% of prison inmates had grown up without a father.

Studies show that one of the major reasons for anger and confusion leading to violence is a sense of separation from father. A father plays an important role in his children's learning to deal with their anger, and in their use of violence as a tool for resolving problems. It is a well-known fact that people who do not see a better solution in a situation typically use violence. When confused and overwhelmed, these people react with violence. One of the most important roles of a father is teaching his children to deal with anger. A child with a positive relationship with his dad is likely to be skilled at resolving conflicts by controlling anger and not resorting to violence. He is usually able to recognize, respect, and work inside of his own feelings as well as those of the other person involved.

The connection between father absence and violent criminals is obvious, just as the connection between violent fathers and violent children is clear. Children learn from their fathers.

Children without fathers suffer from health problems, as well. Reports have shown poorer emotional adjustment often resulting in anxiety. These children living without fathers, especially after divorce, have a 50 percent greater risk of having asthma, frequent headaches, and speech defects (Blankenhorn, 1994). The increase risk of accidents, injuries, and poisonings elevated scores for health disadvantage in comparison to children with two parents. The predicted risk of injury was about a third greater.

As far as academic achievement, children of divorce show early signs of truancy and disengagement from school. They also tend to have a negative attitude towards class and teachers in general. Less monitoring of schoolwork and social activities by the one parent, as compared to an intact family, often results in lower educational expectations and non-existent social activities.

According to statistics, out of all the negative consequences of absent fathers, juvenile delinquency and violence are among the most severe. The following are facts:

- Since 1960, while the population has gone up by only 41 percent, there has been a 550 percent increase in reported violent crime. The segment with the fastest growing crime rate is juveniles.

- Between 1983 and 1992, arrests of juveniles for murder went up by 128 percent.

- Studying two groups of Philadelphia boys, those born in 1945 and the others in 1958, found that the later group was three times more likely to commit violent crimes and five times more likely to commit robberies. These findings parallel the increases in fatherlessness.

- From the National Surveys of Children, a major longitudinal study done in two waves, found that family disruption "was associated with a higher incidence of several behavioral problems, negative effects being greatest with multiple marital transitions."

- Gottfredson and Hirschi in *A General Theory of Crime*, concluded, "such family measures as the percentage of the population divorced, the percentage of households headed by women, and the percentage of unattached individuals in the community are among the most powerful predictors of crime rates."

- Sixty percent of America's rapists, 72 percent of adolescent murderers, and 70 percent of long-term prison inmates come from Fatherless homes.—National Fatherhood Initiative. (Blankenhorn, 1995)

- In 1993 there were 3,647 teenage killers; by 2005, criminologist James Fox expects there will be 6,000 of them. If the number of absent fathers continues to increase, we face even more dangerous times ahead.

4

WHAT IT TAKES TO BE A GOOD FATHER

A good father is not always defined in terms of biological or genetic make-up but in the nature of a male's responsibility, accountability, and involvement with his child, whether male or female. The characteristics of good fathers are exhibited in their caring, sharing, and daring sacrificial life styles toward their offspring. In terms of population, good fathers are very difficult to find compared with the large. percentage of good mothers. Good fathers are also difficult to find when comparing them to the characteristics mentioned: caring, sharing and daring. All three components mentioned, caring, sharing and daring express responsibility, accountability, and reliability.

CARING

First a good father cares in a loving manner to the point of denying himself for the welfare of his children. Fatherly care touches the physical, psychological, emotional, and the spiritual component of a child. The caring by a biological father is deeply rooted in the nature of God our spiritual Father. However, men who are not biological fathers but who are symbols of fatherhood exhibiting care, the ability to share, and daring to be different from the deadbeat fathers, could also be styled as a good father. Such persons symbolizing these qualities mentioned could be an uncle, cousin, or have some other relationship with the child. Also a stepfather could easily bear the characteristics of a good father, caring, sharing, and daring to sacrifice what is needed for the child's survival and qualify as a good father.

The term care is exhibit by love not force. A good father in not made to love his child. For example, natural law does not threaten penalties on the father who does not support his child. The good father cares about what God has blessed him with and feels honored to support his child. One of the most influential studies of paternal impact on the overall socio-emotional development of children was done by developmental psychologists Ann Easterbrooks and Wendy Goldberg, who, after considering dozens of potential influences, such as social class, economic and martial circumstances, child's birth order and gender, concluded that the father's attitudes toward, and behavioral sensitivity to the care of his children have more positive influence on the child's socio-emotional development than the total amount of time spent in interaction with the child.

Bottom line: the closer the connection between father and child, the better off they both are now and in the future (Pruett).

SHARING

Second, a good father shares his love toward his son or daughter, a love that is only surpassed by the love of God for the world. The evidence of the father's sharing is that the child shares in return. The good father shares himself with his child unselfishly, sharing in terms of giving without restraint, particularly of his time together, with all his abilities. As an acting chaplain for a high school football team consisting of approximately fifty players, I have clearly seen that good fathering is not exhibited among the players. With twelve games a season, the percentage of fathers present at each event is extremely low. The coaches, teachers, and I often take on the role of fatherhood for each child who is fatherless. The duties off the field for the coaches, out of the classes for the teachers, as well myself, require sharing additional time in order to help deal with the emotional, psychological, and emotional problems of these children. In contrast to the good father who shares without compromise, the negative father is not supportive, even from a distance. Sharing further expresses responsibility of the father to provide for the needs for the child. Also sharing brings the father into accountability. The child's welfare does the monitoring. If the father is accountable for sharing time, finances, activities etc., he is indeed being a good father.

DARING

Finally, the third component of a good father is to be daring, able to inspire children to actively develop into adulthood. When a father is daring, it shapes the child, making him accept challenges and dare to live his life to the fullest. What some people think cannot be done, the daring father encourages his child to do to step out, and believe in himself. And while the child is stepping out, the father is moving along side of him, cheering the child on. Good fathers are not always genetically connected, but they provide good role models through such programs such as, "Do Something," Best Men, Big Brother, PAL, church activities, etc., which are prevention networks. The PAL (Police Athletes League) involves children in various challenging activities, helping them to avoid the perils of the street and giving them an alternative to gang involvement. "Do Something" is a program designed for middle school children, involving them in character building skills, helping others by doing something worthwhile. Best Men involves the concepts of building boys for manhood, teaching them responsibility, accountability, and reliability to be stable citizens.

5

HELPING FATHERLESS CHILDREN COPE

There are several strategies that are cited for helping fatherless children to cope with the various perils of life.

IDENTIFY THE REALITY OF AN ABSENT FATHER

First, help the child to identify the reality of an absent father. Often children attempt to cover up things that negatively affect them on a daily basis. For example, their behavioral expressions are out of the normal mode of things, such as impoliteness, lack of respect for authority, and lack of interest in learning skills. In most cases, these factors are clear in the life of the fatherless child, but laughter, fights, and the ability to belong cover them up. Teachers, parents, social workers etc., must offer their services in helping the child face this reality, as difficult as it may be. The teacher ought to address this issue, not in a direct or negative manner, but with compassion, wisdom, and much understanding.

IDENTIFY THE REALITY OF THE PRIMARY CARE GIVER

Second, the child can better cope with reality by acknowledging who is the primary caregiver in his life. To help the child cope, explain to him that he must show respect to the primary caregiver in order to progress. We cannot help children cope if the truth is not revealed to them. In order to cope with fatherlessness, the child must be taught the importance of respect.

ACTUATE MORALS BY MODELING

Third, role modeling must actuate morals. It is evident in our society that a small percentage of men attempt to live a holy life before God. In my population, HIV and AIDS are disproportionately damaging the fabric of minority communities. In New Jersey, African American women now account for most new infections. 73.4% of all AIDS cases in Newark are African American. African Americans make up only 25.8% of the total population of the Newark metropolitan area (CDC 1998). We need male role models not only to teach, but also to be a light in this world of darkness. In helping the fatherless to cope, we encourage positive prevention weapons. These weapons tear down the strong holds of the enemy (Satan) who comes to kill, steal, and destroy. Young boys and girls are being killed daily from drugs, gang violence, and HIV. They are being robbed of their youthful years of fun and genuine excitement that God has ordained for them. Robbed of life's beauty. The destroying factor comes when no one has the time to help them cope with their apparent situation of life, fatherlessness.

DIFFERENTIATE REALITY OF FAMILY STRUCTURE

Fourth, to further help fatherless children to cope teach them to differentiate the realities of family structure. The reality of family structure focuses on explaining to children that there are various types of families. For example, families with one parent, the same sex families, and foster families etc. Although we do not agree with the life styles of some families they yet exist. Help the children to understand God intended male and female (father and mother) to raise their children together. However, in the other corner there are those who have tried to prove that fathers are not important at all (Brott, 1999). Children must know emphatically what family structure is now and has always been since God ordained it. The child must understand that he can be victorious in spite of his circumstances and that someone is always willing to help.

DESIGN POSITIVE PROGRAM

Fifth, finally, to help fatherless children cope; designing positive programs is necessary, particularly where male role models are involved. We have many programs offered in the school system in the areas of sports and entertainment, however there are few programs designed to teach values and morals. The ability to teach young middle school boys and girls values and moral standards is very important. Regardless of race, creed, color or religious beliefs, the characteristics of good fathering can be found in uncles, cousins, brothers-in-laws, and friends.

6

CONCLUSIONS AND IMPLICATIONS

Without a doubt, there are many reasons for anger in middle school children. In the majority of cases, some type of dysfunction in the family causes deep-rooted anger and violent behavior. The absence of a father has been proven to have an extremely negative effect on children. It may lead them to engage in violence, sexual promiscuity, and substance abuse. These behaviors stem from anger, which, in many cases, is a general reaction to growing up without a father.

Social analysts believe that many of America's major social problems, such as crime, violent gangs, alcohol and drug use, poverty, low achievement, and marital instability, are attributable to parents splitting and fathers deserting their children. Statistics show that the number of children today who live in a home without a father is incredible. Research has proven that fathers are not expendable. Extensive research shows that fathers are extremely important to children in many ways: economically, socially, scholastically, morally, and spiritually. Involved and responsible fathers bring traits and attitudes to a family, including teaching ways of coping with anger, that have been shown to be very important to the child and society (Manski, et al., 1992). A father who is not involved makes a child think that he is unloved, unworthy or unimportant. This undoubtedly hurts the child's self-esteem, leading to anger or violence issues.

Fathers make proven contributions to the psychological and social development of their children in many ways. Studies indicate that a father's contribution is as essential and irreplaceable as the mother's. Men and women have different parenting techniques and approaches. One approach is not better than the other. Children need interaction from both the mother and father to fully develop and reach their potential.

Typically, fathers tend to be more physical in their parenting techniques, while mothers are more verbal. Fathers encourage their children to take risks while mothers are constantly warning them to be more careful. Fathers are often rougher in playing with children, but psychologists say that this teaches self-control rather than aggression (Popenoe, 1996). Children who are raised without this physical contact with their fathers are more likely to develop aggressive behavior. Specifically, daughters who have physical play with their fathers are more self-confident and assured, while those who do not are more insecure and introverted.

Reestablishing fatherhood has become a significant national trend. From the federal government to the state government, public officials have come to realize the importance of father involvement because it offers two distinct benefits: improvements in the lives of children and substantial cost savings to the system. When states figure out how to increase father involvement, the benefits will be substantial, both in human and economic terms. The potential benefits include: greater protection of children from a broad spectrum of social problems; monetary savings by reducing expenditures on at-risk youth and social programs; increases in child support that will decrease the cost of enforcement measures; decreased poverty among single mothers and children; and enhanced child development in cognitive abilities, social skills, and intelligence.

I know personally of three cases of fatherlessness that caused anger in middle school children and led to tragic results. First, several years ago I had the honor of teaching a fourteen year-old-boy in the eighth grade. I shall call his name John. John entered my class at the beginning of the school year. He began with all of the necessary essentials for class. The few weeks of school John was quite involved with his studies. His work was a bit confusing, but complete. However, after the second month of school, his behavior began to change. I noticed that he would display anger toward other students. Soon fights ensued. John was then asked to bring his parents to school, however only his mother came. Weeks went by. John became very explosive and he would not listen. Finally his father arrived, and he completely changed his behavioral patterns. He was no longer angry. It was clear John needed the presence of his father. To shorten the story, after that the father withdraw himself again because of a conflict with the mother, and John went completely out of control. John left school in May on a Friday and was to return on Monday, but he never returned. He was killed in a drive-by shooting on Saturday noon.

Second, Altraik, not his real name, was a young teenager fifteen years of age, also an eighth grader. He grew up fatherless. Trouble followed him daily. Altraik was very unstable but reachable with the aid of love and compassion. However, he was filled with anger, used profanity, smoked when the teacher left the room, and fought almost every day. I would counsel him regularly concerning his anger. By the end of the school year through much prayer and constant supervision his behavior showed improvement. One year following, Altarik graduated from the eighth grade. Then I read in the newspaper that he had been killed in a drive-by shooting. I contacted Altraik's mother and she confirmed the tragedy had taken place. Months earlier Altraik had become a believer, but was killed on his porch through mistaken identity.

Third, Allen was a pleasant fourteen-year-old, whom I knew since the sixth grade. His mother always accompanied him to school when needed. The father was addicted to drugs and alcohol. Allen experienced much anger. Although it did not surface in the form of violence, it was there. His anger was expressed though neglect. Allen occupied himself with nothing, attempting to get his mother's attention because of his absent father. Allen was given the opportunity to vent with me many times—never violent, but yet angry. Finally Allen graduated from the eighth grade but after the death of his father he fell victim to selling drugs. Allen is still living. He is nineteen, but recently received a three-year sentence in the penitentiary for drug dealing.

These overwhelming personal experiences, coupled with extensive research data, lead me to conclude that the problems associated with father absence are monumental. They create substantial negative consequences, especially anger in middle school children. They need to be better addressed in order to nurture a healthy, productive society. As the number of absent dads has steadily risen over the years, so have statistics on anger and violence in middle school children. It cannot go on.

REFERENCES

Austin, Joe, and Willard, Michael Nevin, eds. (1998). *Generations of Youth: Youth Cultures and History in Twentieth-Century America.* New York: University Press.

Barber, Nigel (2000). *Why Parents Matter: Parental Investment and Child Outcomes.* Greenwood, Westport, Ct. Bergin and Garvey.

Barras, R. Jonetta (2000). *Whatever Happened to Daddy's Little Girl? The Impact of Fatherlessness on Black Women.* New York: Valentine Group Press.

Beck, Allen, Kline, Susan and Greenfield, Lawrence (1998). "Survey of Youth in Custody, *1987,*" *Bureau of Justice Statistics Special Report,* U.S. Department of Justice.

Blankenhorn, D. (1995). *Fatherless America: Confronting our Most Urgent Social Problem. Basic Books.* New York: Harper Collins Publishing Co.

Brody, Leslie (1999). *Gender, Emotion, and the Family.* Cambridge: Harvard University Press.

Brott, A. Armin and Parke, D. Ross (1999). *Throwaway Dads.* New York: Houghton Mifflin Company.

Bumpass, L. and Sweet, J. (1989). *Children's Experience in Single Parent Families: Implications of Cohabitation and Marital Transitions.*Madison, w. Family Planning Perspectives,

Chadwick, Bruce A. and Heaton Tim B. (1988). *Statistical Handbook on the American Family.* Phoenix: Oryx Press.

Coltrane, Scott. (1996). *Family Man: Fatherhood, Housework, and Gender Equity*. New York: Oxford University Press.

Garfinkel, I., McLanahan, S. and Robins, P. (1994). *Child Support and Child Well-Being*. Washington DC: The Urban Institute Press.

Griswold, Robert L. (1993). *Fatherhood in America*: A History. New York: Basic Books.

Hanson, T. (1996). *Does Parental Conflict Explain why Divorce Is Negatively Associated with Child Welfare?* Source: Magazines, Lansdale on Encyclopedia.com 2002.

Hanson, T., McLanahan, S. and Thomson, E. (1997). *Consequences of Growing Up Poor*. Chicago: University of Chicago Press.

Haveman, R., and Wolfe, B. (1994). *Succeeding Generations: On the Effects of Investments in Children*. New York: Russell Sage Foundation.

Levine Beth. (1995). *Divorce–Young People Caught in the Middle*. Berkeley Heights, N.J.: Enslow Publisher.

Lupton, Deborah and Barclay, Lesley. (1997). *Constructing Fatherhood: Discourses and Experiences*. Thousand Oaks: Publisher Sage Publication.

Manski, C., Sandefur, G. McLanahan, S., and Powers, D. (1997). "Alternative Estimates of the Effects of Family Structure During Childhood on High School Graduation." *Journal of the American Statistical Association*.

McLanahan, S. and Booth, K. (1989). "Mother-only Families: Problems, Prospects and Politics." *Journal of Marriage and the Family*.

McLanahan, S. and Sandefur, D. (1994). *Growing Up With a Single Parent*. Massachusetts: Harvard University Press.

Popenoe, D. (1988). *Disturbing the Nest: Family Change and Decline in Modern Societies.* A. De Gruyter.

_____(1996). "Life Without Father." *The Free Press.*

_____(15 Feb,1995) "Crime Wave Forecast With Teenager Boom," *San Francisco Chronicle.*

0-595-30328-5

www.ingramcontent.com/pod-product-compliance
Lightning Source LLC
LaVergne TN
LVHW040905190125
801669LV00006B/100